WISDOM FOR LIFE 101
LIFE-CHANGING PRINCIPLES

AUBREY MORRIS

authorHOUSE®

AuthorHouse™
1663 Liberty Drive
Bloomington, IN 47403
www.authorhouse.com
Phone: 1 (800) 839-8640

© 2016 Aubrey Morris. All rights reserved.

No part of this book may be reproduced, stored in a retrieval system, or transmitted by any means (except for brief quotations) without the written permission of the author.

Published by AuthorHouse 05/16/2016

ISBN: 978-1-5246-0720-3 (sc)
ISBN: 978-1-5246-0721-0 (hc)
ISBN: 978-1-5246-0719-7 (e)

Library of Congress Control Number: 2016907308

Print information available on the last page.

Any people depicted in stock imagery provided by Thinkstock are models, and such images are being used for illustrative purposes only. Certain stock imagery © Thinkstock.

This book is printed on acid-free paper.

Because of the dynamic nature of the Internet, any web addresses or links contained in this book may have changed since publication and may no longer be valid. The views expressed in this work are solely those of the author and do not necessarily reflect the views of the publisher, and the publisher hereby disclaims any responsibility for them.

Scripture quotations marked KJV are from the Holy Bible, King James Version (Authorized Version). First published in 1611. Quoted from the KJV Classic Reference Bible, Copyright © 1983 by The Zondervan Corporation.

Contents Page

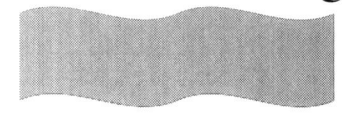

Dedication ix
Acknowledgements xi
Introduction xiii

1 1
2 2
3 3
4 4
5 5
6 8
7 9
8 10
9 11
10 12
11 15
12 16
13 17
14 18
15 19
16 22
17 23
18 24
19 25
20 26
21 29

22	30
23	31
24	32
25	33
26	36
27	37
28	38
29	39
30	40
31	43
32	44
33	45
34	46
35	47
36	50
37	51
38	52
39	53
40	54
41	57
42	58
43	59
44	60
45	61
46	64
47	65
48	66
49	67
50	68
51	71
52	72
53	73
54	74
55	75

56	78
57	79
58	80
59	81
60	82
61	85
62	86
63	87
64	88
65	89
66	92
67	93
68	94
69	95
70	96
71	99
72	100
73	101
74	102
75	103
76	106
77	107
78	108
79	109
80	110
81	113
82	114
83	115
84	116
85	117
86	120
87	121
88	122
89	123

90	124
91	127
92	128
93	129
94	130
95	131
96	134
97	135
98	136
99	137
100	138
101	139
Also by Aubrey Morris	141

Dedication

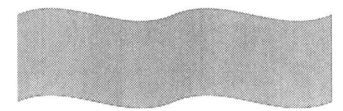

This Wisdom book is dedicated to the memory of Gert Van Wyk and Alec Van Wyk; two of my great spiritual mentors. Both loved and not forgotten.

Acknowledgements

- *To my beautiful family: Auriel, Dillon and Levi; I am blessed and appreciative for your patience and support as I chase my dreams.*

- *Thank you to Paula Kavanagh for the author photo.*

- *Thank you to Tracy Hughes; for your endorsement. Your zest and gusto for life is truly inspiring. Your friendship is priceless.*

- *To Wayne Thring, Collin Govender, Paul Drury and Mike Holohan; you have all been great spiritual mentors and friends. I feel well-grounded. Also to Moses Pillay, Mervin Pillay, Richard Beeson, Marlon Van, Simon Fleming, Rodney McComb and Olugbenga Oluwasanya; your friendship and care is well noted.*

- *To AuthorHouse; Once again, you have all assisted me in producing another wonderful book that will inspire and fortify many who read it. Thank you to: Julius Artwell, Frannie Poulsen, Carlos Cortes, Leigh Allen, Joseph Elas, Primo Santos, Richelle Keith and Michael Green.*

Introduction

A very wise and sacred book called the Bible had these following words to say about wisdom:

"Wisdom is the principal (main) thing; therefore get wisdom: And with all thy (your) getting, get understanding" (Proverbs 4:7) KJV.

It is quite obvious that without wisdom, your life will not be as effective, promising and full. To live without wisdom is like one floundering through life. It is like playing a game of hit and miss. It is like entering a maze and struggling to find the exit.

No one really sets out in life to be dumb, dull, ignorant, short-sighted, and gullible or easily manipulated. No one sets out to live a life that is constantly snow-balling out of control and sync with who he or she really is and purposes to be. Hence, wisdom is crucial in helping you manage your life in such a way that you are a help and benefit to yourself and others. Unwise living can cause unnecessary heart-ache and even loss. Those who lack wisdom can become a liability, instead of an asset to themselves and others.

Everyone needs knowledge, understanding and common sense with regards to all aspects of life; and then the wisdom on how to best use what they know and understand. Wisdom is vital in the stewardship of:

- time management
- relationships
- spiritual and practical aspects
- financial dealings
- health and lifestyle
- careers, aspirations and dreams
- your gifting and talents
- business adventures
- conflict resolution techniques
- parenting

How is wisdom defined? In simple terms, WISDOM is: *to know how to effectively use the knowledge and understanding you gain to your advantage and betterment.* Wisdom can also be defined as possessing: *insight, soundness, prudence, discernment and sapience.*

In the Oxford dictionary, wisdom is defined as: *having good judgement or common sense; being wise; being aware and alert and experienced.*

You can easily tell when someone is unwise, whether it is with their finance, relationships, assets, gifts, health, time, and so on. Wisdom or the lack of it shows up in behaviour, speech, and manner of life. How you live and manage your life indicates your level of wisdom. People, who think they know it all, are unlikely to learn anything new. No one knows everything. That is why we need the counsel of others, which can prove beneficial and life-changing.

Wise people will always seek out wise counsel. It requires that you open your ears and close your mouth. What you have to say, you already know. What others have to say may be new to you. They may bring out things you did not previously know or experience.

No one grows alone, or becomes wise without assistance. There are people constantly feeding richness into your life. Your job is to take it in, assimilate it and let it work for your benefit. So it is wise to acknowledge and accept enlightenment from others, especially in areas of lack in your life. Trust the wisdom of God in others, and lean or rely on God fully. King Solomon, the wisest man who ever lived, said:

"Trust in the Lord with all thine (your) heart; and lean not unto thine (your) own understanding" Proverbs 3:5 (KJV).

Again Solomon tells us in Proverbs 1:5 that a wise man will listen to good instruction and increase in learning. The person who pays attention to wise counsel or advice shows great understanding. Only unwise people reject sound or good counsel. You are safe when you are in the company of wise people who give you sound or reliable advice. Solomon points this out:

"Where no counsel is, the people fall: but in the multitude of counsellors, there is safety" Proverbs 11:14 (KJV).

A person cannot spend great amounts of time in the company of foolish people and expect to be wiser. A wise proverb found in the Bible says:

"He that walketh (associates) with wise men shall be wise: but a companion of fools shall be destroyed (ruined)" Proverbs 13:20 (KJV).

It is a tragedy to be heading for calamity and not even know it. That is why you need wisdom every day for all situations. That term: *"ignorance is bliss"* is not always true. Ignorance regarding certain aspects of life can prove detrimental in many circumstances.

Wisdom will never be your enemy. Wisdom is like a close friend. Wisdom is a graceful and gracious thing. Wisdom helps you see and experience the pleasantness and meaningful side of life in the face of many harsh realities.

Wisdom is strongly likened to an ornament of grace or crown of glory according to Proverbs 4:9 (KJV). In other words, wisdom promotes you and brings honour and stableness to your life. Wisdom beautifies or adorns you. So wisdom is seen as precious treasure. Wisdom enhances you just like jewellery adorns and enhances a person's beauty. Wisdom makes you function the best way. Let wisdom be the seedbed where you cultivate an effective, meaningful and wholesome life.

There is a key to getting wisdom or becoming wise. Learn to listen to and obey good and beneficial instruction. There is wisdom on the lips of parents, teachers, coaches, siblings, friends, employers, doctors, scientists, solicitors and spiritual leaders. Just by listening and then taking on board what they say can enrich your life, and also save you from pitfalls, or from going around the same mountain more times than you need to. This is not to say that people who are wise never make mistakes or do foolish things.

Wisdom needs your co-operation. It cannot work alone. If you do not engage wisdom and the illumination and savviness it brings, then you are likely to remain stunted. I see myself as possessing a good amount of wisdom; but on the other hand I can list all the foolish things I have done. If I had known back then what I know now, I probably would not have engaged in those foolish things.

Because of a lack of wisdom and obedience, the nation of Israel turned a 12 day journey across the desert to the promised land of Canaan into a 40 year wilderness experience. This historical incident is found in the Bible. They were the ones to blame for their wilderness experience, not God. Stubbornness and foolishness come at a high cost, resulting in the squandering of potential and golden opportunities. Point of the matter is that we must flow in the direction of wisdom, not against.

Wisdom matures you, and grounds you. You gain a great respect for life, people, God and the planet. You start to live soberly. You start to see, not only with your eyes, but with your heart as well. You start to value your time, and not let people waste it. Many people waste their time and lives because they do not have the wisdom to search out and tap into their core, or reason for existence.

God has wisdom that He has whole-heartedly agreed to give to those who ask; and it is free. It is His desire for us to be wise and prudent.

"If any of you lack wisdom, ask of God that giveth to all men liberally (freely)" James 1:5 (KJV).

In this transformational book, I have written 101 bite-size messages on WISDOM for life. Each message is fortified and life-changing.

So whether you are relaxed at home with a cup of coffee, or riding on a bus or train, waiting in line for an appointment, or just out on the porch enjoying the afternoon breeze or sun; have this wisdom book within easy reach. I trust it will enrich your life and add value and depth to it. You will be ten times better for it. A reference for this is found in the book of Daniel 1:20.

"And in all matters of wisdom and understanding, that the king inquired of them, he found them to be ten times better than all the magicians and astrologers that were in all his realm (territory)" KJV.

In the words of king Solomon (the wisest man who ever lived), ***"Iron sharpens iron"*** Proverbs 27:17 (KJV).

Allow these 101 bite-size "Wisdom for Life" messages, which are timeless, ageless and life-changing, to sharpen you and impact your life.

"Seek God's will in all you do, and He will show you the path to take." Proverbs 3:6 (NKJV)

*It is time for you to look
forward, not back,
because God is working
on your future,
not your past.
To engage your future, your mind
has to be in forward-
drive, not reverse.
Some people exist to fix their lives
based on their past;
but God wants you to yield your life
to Him based on the future
He has for you.*

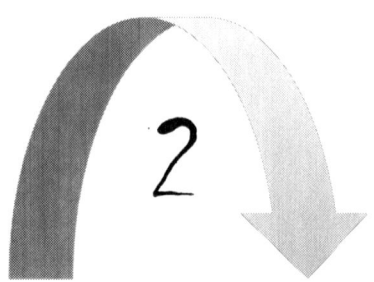

*True strength comes from
daily prayer, hope and patience;
and an unrelenting desire to succeed,
even against the storms of life.
You have life; but now the question is:
Do you want to succeed in life?*

You must live purposefully and passionately; not aimlessly and haphazardly. You must use your God-given potential and creativity to paint the best picture of your life. Remember, you were created to live, not just exist.

*Work at becoming who God
wants you to be and
not what other people
think you should be.
Your purpose comes from God,
and not man. Let God
have the final say.*

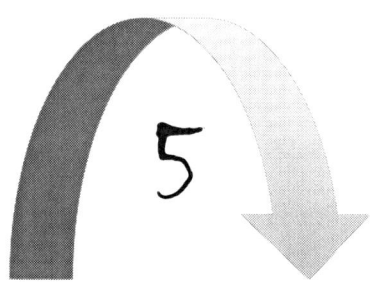

*Take the time to listen to
other wise people,
and not just yourself.
You will be amazed at how
enriched your life
will be when you
allow others to cultivate your life
with seeds (words) of wisdom.*

Reflective Notes

*God took His time
to write us important instructions
in His Holy Bible;
Therefore we should take
the time to read those instructions;
for He offers guidance on
all aspects of life.*

Whatever you set out to do in life;
If you think you CAN'T,
then you WON'T;
But if you think and
believe you CAN,
then you WILL.

The best One to have on your side is God, because He adds value, wholeness and purpose to your life; and only takes away the negative things.

*POWER and WEALTH will
test your CHARACTER.
Your head might be in the clouds
of fame and prestige,
but keep your feet
on the ground. Let God
regulate your power and
influence with humility, so you do not
self-destruct, but advance;
helping others
less fortunate than you are.*

*It is difficult to have
a positive life with a negative mind.
Change your thinking and outlook;
then positivity becomes automatic.
Be the optimist who sees
the 'big picture,'
instead of a pessimist who
sees only the 'negative.'*

Reflective Notes

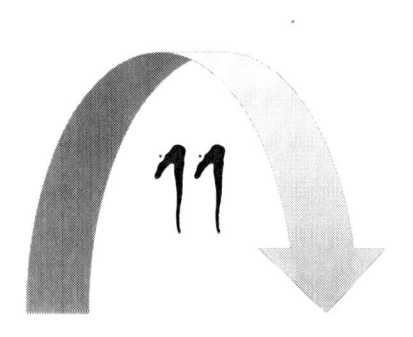

Many people desire to do great things, and impact their generation; but desire without action amounts to nothing. You must engage; you must act. Be the person who DOES GREAT THINGS others talk about; instead of being the person who TALKS ABOUT GREAT THINGS others do.

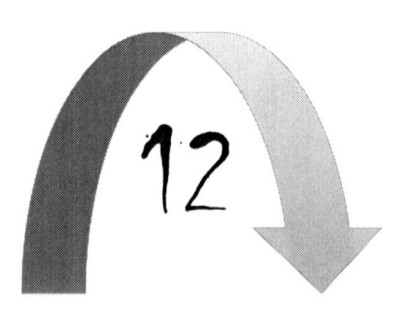

*Do not give up
on your dreams just because
the conditions are not suitable.
Conditions change, so keep dreaming.*

13

*Face each day
With the attitude of a winner,
the fortitude of an over-comer,
and the patience of a runner.
Your life journey is like a marathon,
so pace yourself. You will get there.*

14

*God's Love for you
is greater than all your failures.
So guess where your mind should be?
On God's Love for you.*

15

*When you hit Rock-Bottom,
all you can do is Look Up.
God is there, and He has
great plans for your life.
You have to be utterly convinced
that God wants you to succeed,
even when your circumstances
say otherwise.
Keep your hope alive;
as well as your strength to survive;
by having God in your life.*

Reflective Notes

*You can trust God
with your future, for He
knows everything;
including awesome
plans for your life.
It is about abandoning yourself
to God who will never abandon you.*

17

*When you feed yourself
with a constant diet of
negativity and pessimism,
it is then hard to have
a positive outlook.
There is strength in
hoping for the best,
instead of settling for what is less.*

*As a creation of God,
you do not need other people
to validate your existence and worth.
God has already done that.
Your job is to live confidently
with certainty,
even in the face of obscurity.*

People who talk more about their past and missed opportunities make very little future progress. They live in a stagnant pool of indecisiveness and procrastination. Do not be like a plane that is only circling the runway. At some point you need to take off and fly to your destiny.

*You need persistence to get
what you need in life;
and once you have it, you then need
tenacity to keep what
persistence got you.
Some people give up too
soon, and never
see the manifestation of
their goals and dreams.*

Reflective Notes

*Before you feel good about
everything else,
feel good about yourself.
It is a healthy way of life;
to view yourself in a positive light.
It will help your confidence
and self-esteem.*

Find relationships that empower and propel you forward, and help lift you to new levels; instead of relationships that deplete or drain you. The right people for your life are those who, not only just take, but pour back richly into your life.

Without Valleys, there would be no Mountains. So when you are in the Valley where there is pain, loneliness, or disappointment; remember God is preparing your Mountain Experience, which will be glorious and victorious. So fear no evil in the 'valley of shadows' (Psalm 23:4).

*Take the time to thank the people
who helped you get to where you are.
But don't forget to start
with God, for He is your
Creator, your greatest
supporter, Saviour
and deliverer, and Heavenly Father.*

*God-given Dreams draw you into
your future, not your past.
So never stop dreaming,
for your dreams
are a revelation of God's future plans;
and God's plans for you
are always good.*

Reflective Notes

26

*Negative thinking cannot
produce positive living.
Your actions are primarily
shaped by your thinking
and mind-set. Think well,
because thinking is a
huge part of you. You cannot
get away from it.
It is not so much what
others think of you
that impacts your life;
but rather what
you think about yourself.*

27

*Be overwhelmingly consumed
by all the good things
God says about you,
and does for you;
rather than being consumed
and deflated
by the negative opinions of others.
Peel off every negative
label and allow God to
redefine you according to
His plan and purpose.*

28

Most people are remembered for their great service, rather than great pomp, pride or status in life. Serving others has the undeniable benefits of humility and promotion; while fostering a heart of consideration and compassion for others, and genuine esteem (admiration and respect) for the one who serves; instilled in the hearts of those being served.

29

God expects us to excel in our gifts and talents. In the same breath, He also expects us to be responsible with our abilities, and manage them well by honing our character, not just our gifts. This gives us a balanced life; and makes us a blessing to society, and not a menace.

*Age is not a sign of
maturity or wisdom.
There are a lot of older
people who are
immature and unwise
in their thinking,
speech, actions and manner of life.
In the Bible, Joseph and
Daniel were young men
full of wisdom and maturity
in how they faced
life issues and in how they
managed themselves.
Jesus was only 12 when He displayed
great wisdom and maturity.*

Reflective Notes

*Don't reach the end of your
most pivotal years
and wish you had taken all
the golden opportunities
life presented you.
It is better to have attempted
and failed, than to
have played it all safe, but
with little achievement.
You have only one shot at this life,
So make it count!*

*Present victories are not for you to
rest on, but build on.
There are more mountains to climb
and victories to claim.
Rather, use your present
victories as a springboard
to launch you further ahead.*

*Keep your mind alive with all
possibilities and
expectations; for your
better days are ahead. Go
fully into that which you
are passionate about. Do not
let temporary storms
or setbacks sap your vigour and joy.
You are more than you see; and you
can do more than you
have ever done.*

34

When you have set clear and achievable goals, you need to commit to the goals until they are accomplished. Planning is great, but working the plan is better. When distractions and unnecessary projects show up, say no. Overload can lead to stress and burnout. It is about fulfilling the dreams in your heart, that bring great satisfaction. Trying to fulfil the wishes and wants of others, while ignoring your passions will eventually lead to frustration.

35

You were designed for a Kinetic experience in God, not a Passive existence. Your dreams, plans and ideas need to be larger than life. Never limit your thinking to small-mindedness; for it is a hindrance to expanding who you are. Believe in God and what he deposited inside of you. Become unstoppable in your pursuit of great achievements.

Reflective Notes

36

*Excuses can be a cop-out, discard them.
Pain can be a motivator, use it.
Dreams can be a door to your future, open them.
Michael Jordan said:
"You miss every shot you do not take." You must not miss the wonderful opportunities God brings your way. They may seem small, like that one brick in the wall. But each brick is necessary to make up the entire wall.*

37

It is pointless to have success if it cannot benefit others. We are blessed to be a blessing (Genesis 12:2). To make an impact and be of significance to your generation starts when your achievements and success empower others, making their lives better.

38

You cannot have true success
without applying
wisdom to your life. A lack
of wisdom causes people
to seek only after what is
temporal and perishable,
instead of what is eternal
and incorruptible.
Wise people seek after
treasures that are deeper
than the surface and further
than the horizon.
You have to learn to see
and perceive things
beyond the limitations of
your physical eyes
and current experiences.

*To start something is
good, but the finish
is even better. Many
things can be started,
but the challenge is in having
the time, patience,
determination, effort and
tenacity to endure
the process that leads to that finish.
Wishing cannot bring
you to your destiny.
Action is required on your part.
Accolades, celebrations, and that
satisfaction of something
well done all come
at the finish, not the start.*

40

Have you prepared for what you are about to birth in the next level? Ants do not get ready for winter in winter; Rather they use the previous, warm season to ready themselves for winter. They are wise. People who are wise think beyond today. They think about and prepare for what is next, and not just for what is.

Reflective Notes

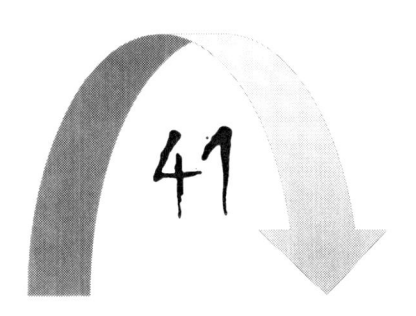

*Wisdom works in a powerful way,
just as much as foolishness
does. Wisdom has the
power to better your life;
whereas foolishness
can ruin your life.
It is just a matter of
which one you allow
to have an effect and an influence
on your life. It is down to choice.*

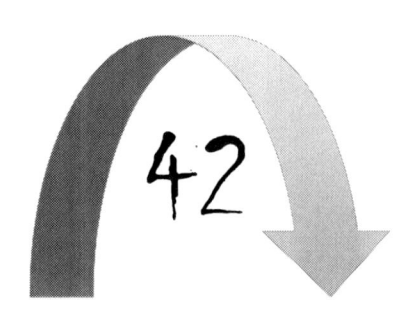

*It is not up to others to fulfil
your destiny for you.
It is your responsibility
and prerogative.
So quit letting people squeeze you into
tracks or patterns you
were not designed for;
especially ones that lead
you away from your
true destiny, instead of to it.*

43

*Just because you cannot
see or feel the sun,
does not mean it is not
there shinning.
The same applies to God.
Just because you may
not see Him, or even feel Him,
does not mean He is not there,
for He is always present.
You are called to a 'faith walk,'
not a 'sight or feel walk'*

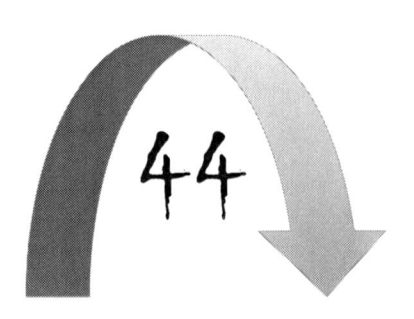

*Purpose is more important than life.
You are alive because of purpose.
God purposed to create
you for a purpose.
So your existence is crucial
to your purpose. It is
tied to your purpose.
Without purpose,
life is pretty meaningless.
Discovering your purpose
nullifies aimlessness, frustration
and insignificance.*

*God did not design you
just to cope with life,
but to overcome in life; for you to be
the head and not the tail; for you
to be above and not beneath; for you
to thrive instead of just
surviving; for you
to shine bright, instead of
cowering away, hidden.*

Reflective Notes

*Some trials and storms are designed
to push you further
towards your destiny.
Have the wisdom to
discern the purpose of
the test, trial or storm that may
be raging in your life.
God has a way of using the things
that have the potential to harm you,
to actually complete you.*

47

If you do not believe you are a great person, capable of attempting and accomplishing great things, you never will. The output of your life is dependant on the input in your life, and your state of mind. A chicken mentality will never elevate you to saw above the clouds like an eagle. So develop an eagle mentality.

*Wise people make an
effort to avoid the
seven things that God hates or detests:*

- *a proud or haughty look*
- *telling lies*
- *killing innocent people*
- *devising wicked and destructive plans*
- *eagerness to do evil or harm*
- *bearing false witness against someone*
- *destroying unity by bringing strife or discord*

49

Brash and hurtful words can furrow deep wounds in the soul, which take years to heal. Wisdom is therefore required when we speak to others; especially when we are angry, upset or in the wrong frame of mind. It is nearly impossible to take back thoughts that have been made public by your tongue.

50

Wisdom is not something you confess, but possess. It is something you can own. If you have it, it will then reveal itself in your speech, actions and attitude. It will preserve you through the many challenges and complexities of life.

Reflective Notes

*On your journey in life,
you do not want
a tired mind, a tired body
and tattered emotions.
Rest periods are vital. Take
time to rejuvenate.
It is not a waste of time,
but a necessity of life.
You are no good to yourself or others
if you are frazzled or burnt out.*

*Your significance and value
does not come from
what you do, but rather
from who you are.
You are a master-piece
created by God.
Your authenticity has
already been validated.
Being who you are is sufficient.
Doing what you do is just a bonus.*

53

As a human being, you
are more precious to
God than all the stars, galaxies
and heavenly bodies.
If God calls the stars by name;
how much more you?
Many times you see greatness,
value and beauty
in others, but often forget
about the greatness,
value and beauty in yourself.
There will always be
others more beautiful or
capable than you are,
BUT they can NEVER BE YOU.
You are one of a kind.

54

*You must endeavour to
care more for people
than for things. Things
can be replaced,
but people cannot, for
they are unique.
Things cannot respond to you with
love, joy, appreciation,
care and friendship,
like people do. It is the
warmth of companionship
and other levels of human
interaction that
complete you, and draw
the best out of you.*

*The world needs what good
you have to offer.
If you do not, it borders on
selfishness and apathy.
You were designed to be
society's answer, and not
society's problem or burden.
Your gifts and abilities
are not just for you, but for others too.
When others are able to
shine brighter because of
you; then your light has
genuine purpose.*

Reflective Notes

56

*Find the good seeds in your life, and bring them to life, initiating growth, and then a beautiful, fruitful harvest.
As for the bad seeds; ignore them and let them remain forever dormant.*

*Leaders who are pessimistic
and cynical
will seldom motivate
those under them
to produce or function
at their optimum.
People need to be motivated,
encouraged.
and inspired to produce their best.
This is only achieved by
optimistic and enthusiastic
leaders, who remain highly positive
in the face of mediocrity
and negativity.*

*Do not alter yourself just to get
people to love and accept you.
Discard that false or
super embellished
and unrealistic identity.
Remain your original self; and the
right people will love,
appreciate and accept you.*

59

When you feel life dragging you down, surround yourself with people who will lift you up. Remember your mountain experiences for encouragement during your valley moments; realizing that circumstances are subject to change. The storms do not last forever. You can rise again.

*Find people who speak life
and truth to you.
Find people who are honest
and trust worthy.
Find people who have your
best interests at heart.
You need people who
will complete you,
not people who will deplete you.
Point of the message is to
help you exercise wisdom
in choosing the people
you hang out with;
for they have a greater effect on you.*

Reflective Notes

61

*Helping, respecting and
caring for people
will never go out of fashion.
Keep doing this; for it
offers people hope,
joy, love and a sense of well-being
against the harsh realities of life;
while keeping you
grounded, humbled,
and tender-hearted.*

*You do not need permission
from people to
be authentic, original,
unique and amazing.
God already wired that to your DNA.
Normality or mediocracy
is not your portion.
Embrace and live out your greatness,
irrespective of who fails to see it.*

63

*Accepting help when
you need it is NOT
a sign of weakness, but a
display of wisdom.
For, to possess wisdom does not mean
you know everything,
but that you are
willing to learn and grow,
by 'sitting at the feet' of
those wiser than you.*

64

*Comfort zones never produce
anything new or
different. You have to
get out of the boat
and step into the new and unknown,
and experience more of
your divine and
awesome destiny; as you
are led and guided
by the unseen hand of God.*

65

To garner (amass or accumulate) a life of significance, effectiveness and influence, you need to spend more time improving your life, rather than entertaining yourself or wishing yourself well; which leads to passiveness and coasting.

Reflective Notes

*Do not be afraid to fail.
Many famous and
successful people did.
The difference is that
they did not give up.
If you find you have been
handed 'lemons;'
turn them into lemonade.
Make the best
out of bad situations or failure.*

*Choice requires wisdom;
because not everything
that looks good
is necessarily beneficial for you.
It is about doing what
is best and right,
that leads to satisfaction,
reward and increase.
No one wants to expend
their energy on things
that diminish who they really are.*

68

*To leaders and parents:
It is good to have your
affairs in order.
It is one thing for your loved
ones to grieve your loss
when you die, but quite
another if they have to
inherit your bills, debt and
unsorted business as well.
Think beyond you; think of
those who depend on you.
Leave a good and lasting legacy that
encourages hope in those
who follow behind.*

It is pointless to have a healthy body, but a troubled mind and emotions that are in tatters. Many people are held back or imprisoned more by being sick in the mind than in the body. A person cannot truly advance with a poor soul even if his or her body is well.

70

Competition can be healthy, where competitors are challenged to do better. However, do not allow it to bring discouragement, despair or contention; where people go to great lengths to outdo each other in a negative manner. Naturally people want to win in life. No one wants to lose all the time, but the key is to remain humble and help others. There should be a genuine desire to see others prosper.

Reflective Notes

71

*The true test of character
is to give a man power.
When some people are thrust
into high positions they
become arrogant, cold and
indifferent, instead
of becoming humble, kind
and understanding.
The higher you go, the more
you ought to take on
humility. Pride and arrogance
only set you up
for a bad crash all the way down.*

*Good character affirms our
values and morals;
and tends to draw the best out of us.
With good character,
people will not go out
of their way to harm
others or become
irresponsible, unreliable or dishonest.
Good character enhances
relationships,
and makes for a better
people and society.*

Serving is one of the major, key aspects in life. It does not matter how large and influential an organization is; if no one serves, that organization will fall apart. Every service causes the 'wheels of the earth' to turn. Whether you serve in the lime-light or backstage, your service is of great importance.

74

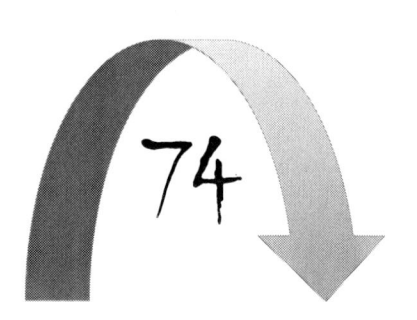

*A dark, tunnel experience should not
stop your forward momentum;
for you know there is always light
at the end of the tunnel.
So keep stepping.
Keep the vision of light in your heart,
even though your eyes
do not see it yet.*

75

Excellence makes for a good reputation. How you present yourself says a lot about you. Package yourself in such a way that you are appealing to others. Then they can taste of all the good substance you have to offer that is beyond your exterior.

Reflective Notes

*Chaos and disorder are
strong hindrances
to progress, harmony and success.
Order and discipline create a pattern
of harmony and focus that lead
to success and advancement;
and this applies
to every arena of your life.
Even God does things in
order and decency.*

77

*Do not expend your energy
on things you cannot change.
Rather do something about
things you can change.
No one is expecting more
than that from you.*

78

It is pointless trying to have a great reputation without great character. Work on your character, and your reputation will prove sweet. Remember, your character is like the building blocks for your reputation.

79

*No one has ever truly
garnered greatness
from belittling other people.
When you serve, uplift
and honour others;
you actually increase
your significance,
greatness and influence
in a positive way.*

80

Do not waste your time trying to prove to people your goodness, worth and authenticity. Just be authentic and just do good.
Let your actions and reputation speak for you.

Reflective Notes

All you have is today.
Tomorrow is not promised to you;
and yesterday is no longer yours.

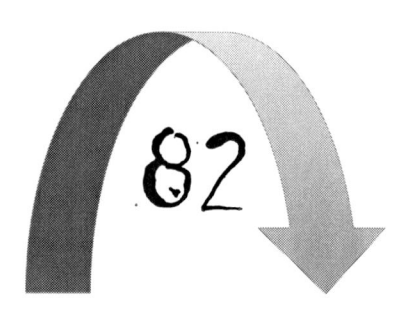

Whatever energizes and excites you, and fuels your passion, is what you should pursue. Let such things have your time and your energy and focus. Everything else is secondary.

83

*If you ever end up where you do not want to be; check your actions and choices.
Many people want the better things in life, but fail to do the things that will help them attain those better things.*

84

*The scars you bare speak
of the wounds
and hurts you endured.
Now you have a story to tell.
A story that says: I was
crushed but not destroyed;
I was wounded but I survived.
Wear your scars with pride.*

Boredom is the door to stagnation and listlessness. Stay curious and adventurous; which is a catalyst for drawing you into greater and new things.

Reflective Notes

*Wisdom allows you to overlook
the things that are trivial,
so you will not be distracted by them.
Rather, give your attention
to those things that
are paramount and life changing.*

When making life-changing decisions, don't rush; and don't seek advice from people who do not share your interests or value your life principles. Find a council of people who are passionate about your goals, your dreams and your success.

If you do not apply what you know, you are seen as just smart; but if you apply what you know, consistently adjusting and correcting things as you go along, then you are moving from being smart to being WISE.

89

*Remember, wisdom
grows in you when
you learn from your experiences;
not just from accumulating them.
Each experience should
be a stepping stone
to a better life for you, irrespective
of the nature of the experience.*

*People who place significant
value and attention
on things that matter in
life; like relationships,
spirituality and personal
growth, show
a deeper level of wisdom.
This leads them to
live life beyond the superficial
attractions of success.
They seek to remain true to
who they are and add
value to themselves and
others, and endeavour
to leave a lasting and
inspiring legacy.*

Reflective Notes

91

With wisdom you can easily squash harmful drama and volatile situations; whilst causing potentially positive things to grow and glow. Unwise people tend to turn a mole hill into a mountain or volcano.

92

*True wisdom is displayed
in you when you
freely use all you know and
understand for the
benefit of others; and
not just yourself.
It is so much more than
just generosity on a
monetary level, because
wisdom is priceless.
You are sharing with others,
not just what you
possess, but who and what you are.*

93

*Wisdom enables you to see beyond your limited and present circumstances.
You see the endless possibilities and opportunities
that spark and fuel creativity that is often hampered when you focus only on your present limitations.*

The people under you will do better when you lead with vigour, gracefulness, passion and optimism; rather than with apathy, arrogance, fear and pessimism. Remember, as a leader people tend to assimilate what you cultivate.

*The true test of great leadership is in how you influence people and advance them; rather than controlling or manipulating them.
Only poor and misguided leaders oppress people.
Great and wise leaders liberate them.*

Reflective Notes

96

*True freedom, happiness
and fulfilment
come from doing what you
know you were born to
do, and not what others
coerce or force you to do.
Be certain of what God
deposited in you,
and have the confidence
and audacity
to live it out, irrespective of what
others say or think of you.*

97

There is much to learn from Worker Bees:
- *They clean the hive.*
- *They search for nectar.*
- *They help pollinate flowers.*
- *They feed the young bees.*
- *They keep the hive at the right temperature.*
- *They defend the hive by stinging the enemy.*

They do all this within their 6 week life span. The question is: What are you doing with your life which is way more than a 6 week span.

98

Share your love, care, resources, knowledge and understanding. It may be someone's bridge to success, or someone's lifeline. You never know the impact of your reach. So reach as far as you can with the best you have to offer.

*Do not limit your sight to
your natural eyes only.
You can see with your
heart; with your spirit;
things that are sacred
and life-changing;
things that are beyond the
realm of natural sight.*

100

*For the world to change,
people have to change.
It is pointless trying to
change the world without
changing yourself or
helping others change.
Be the change you want
to see, and others
will see the change you want.*

101

*In dying, you die once; in living you live every day; so think more about living than dying.
Live, laugh, cry, work, unite, worship, pray play, eat, exercise, study, read, sing, dance...
the list is endless...*

Reflective Notes

Also by Aubrey Morris:

Book: The Potential of Your Life

Available on: Amazon, Barnes & Nobel & AuthorHouse Publishers

For more information or book orders, contact:

- AuthorHouse, 1663 Liberty Drive, Bloomington, IN 47403
  Website: www.authorhouse.com

- Author: Aubrey Morris, 00353834624388
  Email: morrisaubs@yahoo.ie
  Twitter: @morrisaubs
  LinkedIn : https://ie.linkedin.com/in/aubrey-morris-59a0b3a6

Books Avaiable at: *AuthorHouse, Amazon, Barnes & Nobel, and other media outlets.*

Guest Speaking Engagements, Contact:

Aubrey Morris: 00353834624388

Auriel Morris (Personal assistant): 00353862181888

Lightning Source UK Ltd.
Milton Keynes UK
UKOW02n1339210616

276775UK00003B/21/P